THE DANCER'S SON

THE DANCER'S SON

Graham McLanachan

ARTHUR H. STOCKWELL LTD
Torrs Park, Ilfracombe, Devon, EX34 8BA
Established 1898
www.ahstockwell.co.uk

© *Graham McLanachan, 2021*
First published in Great Britain, 2021

The moral rights of the author have been asserted.

All rights reserved.
No part of this publication may be reproduced
or transmitted in any form or by any means,
electronic or mechanical, including photocopy,
recording, or any information storage and
retrieval system, without permission
in writing from the copyright holder.

British Library Cataloguing-in-Publication Data.
A catalogue record for this book is available
from the British Library.

By the same author:
Proverbs and Other Poems
The Time of Singing
The True Church
Surprised by Peace
Our Life
Vespers Music

O Dio, nella tua eredità
　sono entrate le genti:
hanno profanato
　il tuo santo tempio,
hanno ridotto Gerusalemme
　in macerie.

ISBN 978-0-7223-5113-0
Printed in Great Britain by
Arthur H. Stockwell Ltd
Torrs Park　Ilfracombe
Devon　EX34 8BA

CONTENTS

Europa	7
Wrath of the Angel	8
Burning Tower	10
Her Shame	11
Elderly Lady	12
Gloss	13
Petit déjeuner	14
On Holiday to Italy	16
Arcady	17
Melpomene's Complaint	18
A Twenty-second Set of Proverbs	19
When Franz and Marie	21
British	22
Our Time	23
A Proposal	24
Out of the West	25
Fellow-Poet	26
Aged Tyrant	27
Her Day Out	28
Department Store	29
The Snow Blows In	30
A Twenty-third Set of Proverbs	31
Concert Hall	33
Eastern Maxim	34
Her Questions	35
Dionysus	36
Response	37
Whatever Comes	38
Brought Me	39
For Ever There	40
Green Hill at Twilight	41
Widower	42
A Twenty-fourth Set of Proverbs	43
The Dancer's Son	45

Snatches	46
She that was in both Street and Field	47
Painting by D. G. Rossetti	48
Portrait by Lorenzo Lotto	49
Painting by Leonard McComb	50
Portrait by Paul Cézanne	51
Painting by Georges Seurat	52
Line of T. S. Eliot	53
Blue Poles	54
A Twenty-fifth Set of Proverbs	55
Painted Chamber	57
Concert-goer	58
Aesthete	59
Puzzlement of a European	60
Now	61
Treasures in Heaven	62
Saw You	63
Adam	64
Steeple	65
New Name	66
A Twenty-sixth Set of Proverbs	67
I Knelt Down Suddenly	69
I Shall Wade Out	70
I Gazed Up at Stars	71
Homecoming	72
Late Poet	73
To a Lady	74
To Monsieur Bonnard	75
To a Banana	76
Notes	77

Europa

    But when he arrived avid of abduction
    Metamorphosed
    Into the handsomest of bulls
    Her companions told him
    Tearfully told him

    Of her death

Wrath of the Angel

Forty young men one night in Ravenna
Entered a car park
And lay down to sleep
Syrians Somalis Liberians Libyans
And a Moroccan

An angel of San Vitale seeing them
Left his mosaic
For the house of the mayor
Accosting her in her bed
And saying:
'What is this
That thou hast done?'
The woman terrified protested her innocence
Claiming to have absolutely
Nothing to do
With admissions into Italy citing the Dublin
Treaty Geneva
Convention citing
The Dublin Treaty

The angel made no reply and left her

He flew to the car park coming to rest
Over where the youths were
He gave a great cry
Which woke all Ravenna but not the young men
Who on the contrary fell
Into a deeper sleep
And when they awoke they were astonished to find themselves
No longer in Europe
But in Morocco Libya
Liberia Somalia in Morocco Libya
Liberia Somalia

And in Syria

Burning Tower

    Official death-toll final and official
    Seventy-two

    Seventy-two
    Not seventy-three
    A further victim being omitted from the roll
    Additional victim
    Excluded from the roll
    Loveliest of girls
    The victims' victim
    Her name

    Europa

Her Shame

Fatuous survey which had dropped on to the mat:
Was she proud
To be British?

Proud to be British?
Proud to be daughter
Of that impressive race
Which had handed over its patrimony to strangers
Had believed that it had rights
Where no rights were
Had insisted upon taking what it did not own
What was not for the taking:
Its life
Own life?

Portrait of Mr Burke reproduced in her book
Was in the National
Collection
She could see it easily but would make no attempt
Could see it so easily
But would make no attempt
Ashamed
Too ashamed

To look at him

Elderly Lady

She wondered sometimes how her life might have been
Had the world of father
And mother survived

The homogeneity
Narrative shared

Had the space endured which had been her parents'
Country survived
Which she might have been able
To call home

She wondered sometimes how her life might have been
Under different circumstances
Not the broken
Unrecognizable

Under different circumstances

Gloss

Wild-eyed youth accosted me
And said:
'Want a gloss on our National Anthem?

God save our gracious Queen
As she graciously watches
The suicide of her realm
And nobly repeats the words which decadents
Place in her mouth
Victorious and vanquished
Happy and wretched
Glorious as only an accomplice can be
Long to reign over us
Long to reign over us
'We' who are no longer

God save the Queen!'

Petit déjeuner

We sat down at a table on the shaded terrace
And Denis after ordering
Coffee and cakes
Turned to me
And said:
'But how for Europe could it be 'business as usual'
In the period's wake
Nineteen fourteen
To nineteen forty-five?

And what does it matter if France is now
A land of mosques
Simply the northern
Transmarine zone of Algeria?
She was dead already
Dead as the rest
Of western Europe dead from exhaustion
And that is why
What has happened
Has happened'

A waitress appeared with coffee and *madeleines*

My friend looked at me
In expectation
How should I respond? Did I wish to do so
Wish even wish
To do so?
Eventually I said:
'Dead already dead from exhaustion
Is that how you see yourself
See yourself Denis?
Yourself me and across the continent
A multitude of our fellows
Across the continent
Numberless
And unbowed
Multitude

Of our fellows?'

On Holiday to Italy

Said Mr Jaundiced
To his wife:
'Let's go on holiday to Italy
Where a Sri Lankan chef
Will cook our *pasta*
And Punjabi waitress serve it

Let's go on holiday to Italy!
Let's pay out thousands
Of pounds to move
From one dead land to another

Let's go on holiday to Italy!
What lovelier than to visit
A country which no one
Any longer

Can visit!'

Arcady

    And to the agent who persists in wishing to send me
    To Peloponnesian hills:
    'With Mnemosyne the only Arcady
    Only Arcady now To Mnemosyne send me
    Send me

    To where she is!'

Melpomene's Complaint

They thrived grew rich and forsook me!

Fear which I inspire
Had protected them for centuries
But they thrived
Grew rich
And forsook me

Even their sentries along the walls
Have feather beds
Increasingly often
Gates are left open Disbelieving wolves
Approach
And enter

They fail to appreciate the ineluctability
Fail to perceive
Behind abandoned Melpomene

My sister Nemesis

A Twenty-second Set of Proverbs

i
And from the New Age
A cry:
'Trespassers against us we shall pursue at law
And pursue without rest

Pursue and destroy!'

ii
Win the war
And Invasion loses
Lose the peace

And Invasion wins

iii
No figures in the Image which wishes to invite
The figures

Will be ourselves

iv
My muse returning will be a girl much changed
And what I shall write for her
What I shall write for her

The Father only knows

v
Half a century since the Abbot became a monk?
Franz your fiddle!
Joseph your keyboard!
And boys

Your voices!

vi
Let me sit in the Almond with the God-Man!
Let new life

Be mine!

vii
Only success
Survival to cry
(And preferably in song):

'Gloria in excelsis Deo!'

viii
And what shall we do what shall we do
On this 'eighth day
Of the week'?

Don't ask!

ix
Nine discs necessary I think for the sonatas
As for variations
Bagatelles and the rest

We'll see

When Franz and Marie

Arrived in Italy
They did
Just that

And when in the poets they immersed themselves
They did so in an Italy
Just as Italian
As the one which Dante as the one which Petrarch
Had known

Marie and Franz
How remote from us
Franz and Marie

O how remote from us!

British

Proud to exemplify a meaningless category
Which any
Might occupy

Proud of our values decadent values
And of our treacherous
Will

Proud to be British!

Our Time

    Invaders seize and recast in their image
    The historical record

    Decadents inherit
    The Civilized Museum

    And insult her

A Proposal

        And as for what's left of the civilization
        For the *coup de grâce*
        We'll need a mask

        And the mask which I propose
        Feint which I propose

        Is 'War on Racism'

Out of the West

    We remember Poitiers Lepanto Vienna

    And cry out
    Weep
    Tear our clothes
    Black dust sprinkle upon our heads

    Towards heaven!

Fellow-Poet

Wrote to me
Saying:
'Malice not always daughter of Intelligence
As she
Madam Deceit
Has recently reminded me

Lachrymose imbecile emotionally dependent
Upon a *concierge*
What has she gained?
We no longer speak and the work which she invited
Neighbours to deride
(Neighbours who may not have done)
You and her superiors
Her far far superiors

Have admired'

Aged Tyrant

      Must soon depart
      And when she does
      Her court will disperse
      Servants feeble as she is strong
      Will simply
      Scatter

      Aged tyrant must soon disappear
      And when she does

      Her evil will also

Her Day Out

Exhibitions in the morning and afternoon
In the evening
A concert
And if on her circuit she were to find a church
In which to spend
A thankful moment
How lovely!

But why 'how lovely'?
And where this necessity?
Why did she not recognize Gallery and Concert Hall
As churches and as the greatest
As churches
And as the greatest

As cathedrals?

Department Store

Appeared to me
And said:
'My first floor Thought not women's shoes
My second Music
Not men's briefs
My third floor Painting not cork mats
Nor travelling rugs
Nor rocking-chairs

My dust Gold and doors wide open
Ashes Gold
And doors wide open
Come! Come in! Come in! Come!

Come in!'

The Snow Blows In

From Siberia

No train up to town
Nor meal in a restaurant
Nor concert at the Cadogan

Only that experience so much more valuable
Than fulfilment
Of desire:
Being brought face to face with herself
And with her life

In the world

A Twenty-third Set of Proverbs

i
Slaughter
Prepare
And bury her with me
That I might offer a feast

In the Hereafter

ii
Disquieting book?
Perhaps
Perhaps
But no peace

Until we've read it

iii
Smiling before he died: 'I kept faith with the vision
Kept faith with the vision
Vouchsafed

In my youth'

iv
O that all of the squares were as green
As green and with-tree

As Piazza Cavour!

v
Promise never to play it on anything
But a Pleyel
Of *circa* 1836

And you may have my poem

vi
And we remember those noblemen called to be saints
Who rid themselves
Of their land

Of all of their land!

vii
She has slept must have slept remembering her dream

Has slept
Must have slept

And may rejoice!

viii
Man
Lion
Ox
Eagle

The only reading!

ix
Our Magi's Journey quest for Christ
Time
Trials

And final discovery!

Concert Hall

For most if not all of the time
The Maiden

(All of the time
Now unrealistic
Regular irruption of whores inevitable
To make their noise)

Tragic surely that She who was Mistress
Of lands and cities
Should be so reduced
But undismayed I opt for joy
For grateful savouring
Of a priceless gift
Confident that She will see me out
That I shall never know
Shall never experience
That eternal Good Friday which is total absence
Of Herself

For most if not all and thanks be to God
For most of the time

The Maiden

Eastern Maxim

'Be the change you wish to see'
A saintly Indian
Was wont to say

And fascist groups in Europe and America
Have adopted his words

As their motto

Her Questions

Why was she dwelling obsessively upon an instance
Of aggression sustained
So long ago?
It might have become an obsession at any
Or at several moments
Over the years
Why now?

And why was obsession always with adversity
With adversity never
Never with the joys?

Why now?
Why now?

And why never with His blessings?

Dionysus

> Murder
> Banishment
> Neither
> An option
> So love the pact embrace
> The pact
>
> Which you must make with him

Response

Better far better never to have appeared?
Infinitely preferable
Never to have existed?
But we did and we do godless professor
And why?
Why?

Please look at these roses of the Volksgarten
Gold and red roses
Of the Volksgarten
While I pen a few lines which I shall present
Few lines in hope
Hope that you might say:
„Schön
Schön
Ja

Sehr schön!"

Whatever Comes

>Out Expectation! And Demand out out!
>I shall embrace
>Whatever comes
>
>Wind in the south and we shall not have a northerly
>Our visitor Peter
>And we shall not have Paul
>Out Expectation! And Demand out out!
>Let me embrace
>
>Whatever comes!

Brought Me

To Great Art the train to Ravenna brought me
(To the Greatest Art
Train to Ravenna!)
But also to two in the carriage sitting
To fellow-passengers
Opposite me sitting
Young boy and girl all Sweetness and Beginning

To a young boy and girl

For Ever There

    We come away come away perpetually must come away
    But come away in body
    In body come away
    In spirit

    For ever there!

Green Hill at Twilight

The old man descends
Entered him young
And has never left

And the maiden Dusk young as he then was
Reveals his hill
To be the world's most
World's most and nothing else greater

And reveals herself
To be as final only
As light of morning final only
As the dawn which will break
New day which will begin

Above his head

Widower

He sat down on a bench amid sycamores

Never love
Like his love
For the beautiful Caterina
Nor grief so desperate as his
Upon her death

So how to account for this morning's feelings?
How to account
For this nameless excitement
Stirrings which the tall trees seemed to acknowledge
Excitement which the sycamores
Seemed to acknowledge

Smiling?

A Twenty-fourth Set of Proverbs

i
Artist in a hole? Should leave his digging
Climb out into the light

And throw away his spade?

ii
Conscious of irreparability they declare the ruins
A preferable home
Far preferable home

To the old house

iii
As if a 'relationship' were the solution
Solution

And not the problem!

iv
But snap which I took of the Neonian Baptistery
Is picture of a palm
Of red blooms

And shadow!

v
The fairest youth: Survival

vi
Poetry: speaking truth to Decadence

vii
But how can „Kreuzige!
Kreuzige!"

Have the loveliest music?

viii
And God bless the little boy who requests my opinion
Of his new shirt:
His employers have chosen

To train him as a manager

ix
Write to lay your writings
Only
To lay your writings

Upon an altar!

The Dancer's Son

But maybe hope gleams and maybe we can count
Upon a friend in the East
The dancer's son
Child of that girl in a blue dress whirling
In the pine-besieged house

And maybe he will stir arise and come to us
Confounding on his path
The foreign invader
His rest taking only upon reaching the sea
Atlantic blue
As a maternal dress

And when he looks back he will look over nations
Restored and over peoples
Dancing their thankfulness
Before through them moving
Through them returning

To his forest home

Snatches

i
'Our Law School ancient Law School academic
Pride
And joy!'

'Pride and joy? Pride? Joy?
At being so quarrelsome
So degenerate and quarrelsome

That we needed lawyers!'

ii
'Digging yourself into a hole?'

'Hole I'm digging
Is the one which the Father

Wishes me to dig'

iii
'And what did He say what did He say to you
In your April
Vision?'

'That in our final home we shall be able to identify
With the Public Space
Which Space He assured me

Will be ours'

She that was in both Street and Field

Has gone indoors
Retired indoors
To be with Creation's fruits that last

And she that was in the open air
She that outdoors
Was everywhere
Has entered the Library Hall Museum
To be at the end
Among her children

She that was in both street and field
And as we thought
So complacently thought
There eternally to be

Has gone indoors

Painting by D. G. Rossetti
(*The Adoration,* watercolour on paper, 1858-64, Tate)

        Let them visit together visit together
        Both high and low
        Gentile and Jew
        But by deputation just one king
        And just one shepherd
        With Joseph

        And as for raiment let the king be a king
        Shepherd a shepherd
        But Joseph no joiner
        My surrogate no joiner
        But habited brother

        Let them worship together worship together
        Both rich and poor
        Mighty and meek
        But by deputation
        By deputation
        That the number of men of males adoring

        Might be My number

Portrait by Lorenzo Lotto
(*Triple Portrait of a Goldsmith [Bartolomeo Carpan?]*,
oil on canvas, c.1530, Kunsthistorisches Museum, Vienna)

        Box of rings little box in your hand
        Proclaims
        Your art
        But who the goldsmith goldsmith
        Here?

        Your Maker
        Handsome Bartolomeo
        Your Maker thrice-handsome
        Bartolomeo
        And you
        You
        You

        The gold!

Painting by Leonard McComb
(*Mediterranean Sea*, oil on canvas, 2001-2, Royal Academy of Arts, London)

Verticals see as well as levels!
Green and mauve see
As well as blue
Emerald and mauve
The richness see
The inexhaustible!

And no sea none of little armadas
A few boats sinking
Most reaching shore
No Death's herald marine harbinger
Not his trumpet's
Sound
At all

A particular place I have no doubt
I could find out where
Go there and see
More or less what the artist that day saw
A particular place
I'm sure I'm sure
But also essential more importantly essential
Europe's South Sea
Her ideal space
Four-headed waters and ideal space
Our vision

Of Paradise

Portrait by Paul Cézanne
(*Madame Cézanne in a Red Armchair,* oil on canvas, c.1877, Museum of Fine Arts, Boston)

Aged Europe as young as ever
As inventive vital
And young as ever
And Eldest Daughter Church's Eldest
Not so old
That you cannot still leap
With ease still leap over your mother's houses
St-Sauveur
St-Jean-de-Malte
Ste-Marie-Madeleine

Clio may already have whispered a prophecy
But still you dance
Indefatigably dance
And nothing could be further removed from your heart

Than the tomb

Painting by Georges Seurat
(*The Channel of Gravelines, Grand Fort-Philippe*, oil on canvas, 1890, National Gallery, London)

What do the stream and little houses say?
That the vacancy beneath them
Pale gold beneath them
Is sand

And what do the masts and lofty flag-pole say?
That the vacancy around them
Blue-mauve around them
Is sky

And what do I standing before you say?
What
Do I say?

That your vacancy is fullness
Your silence
Music
And your stillness dance serene motionless dance

Of the angels

Line of T. S. Eliot
('The poetry does not matter.')

        And how do I imagine her
        This poetry
        Which 'does not matter'?

        As substance I imagine her
        As substance
        Of what she says
        What she is being overwhelmingly
        Overpoweringly
        What she says
        What she says
        Poetry
        The Poetry
        Girl who matters matters greatly
        And signifies

        For what she says

Blue Poles

    Whose procession are you? You pass without saying
    Caesar's? The Magi's?
    You pass over
    Without saying

    Ribbons tied to you and which blow in the blizzard's
    Motley might have told me
    But I see
    No heraldry

    No matter no matter I shall call you the Saviour's
    Shall baptize you Christ's
    Triumphal
    Procession

    As I climb
    The last of you
    Gazing down
    Upon waters

    Of the incoming
    Tide

A Twenty-fifth Set of Proverbs

i
Dictator's ghost seeing domes and towers
Smiled:

'Others are completing my work'

ii
Politician and journalist
Fell upon the patriot

And killed him

iii
Church's sanctuary but they may murder us anyway
As they murdered Berthefried
Killed

Poor Berthefried!

iv
And at a window high in the tower inscribed
'Liberal Left'
Virtue appeared
Pushed open the window
And cried:

'Save me!'

v
Life of the Body?
Life's house

Has no life

vi
Success
Escape
Success
Escape
Success
Uniquely

Escape!

vii
And all that the worldlings new worldlings do?

Return us to the desert
Return us to that desert
Where we first

Heard God's word!

viii
Wrestlers in the Hell-ring but proud proud
And no pride

Like ours!

ix
Orchard César would bring back:
'Beautiful

Beautiful as a church!'

Painted Chamber

But what does the letter contain which the marquis
Is holding?
Who is the figure to his right?
What are they saying
And how does the fresco
Relate to another relate if at all to another
In the room?

Little girl dare not bite into her apple
Without Mama's consent
Francesco cardinal newly appointed
Holds a younger
Brother's hand
Who holds a still younger nephew's hand
And portraiture includes
Insists upon including
Dogs
And a dwarf

What shall I retain? Unanswerable questions?
And what shall I retain?
Inappropriate questions

Or image of informality
Hymn to tenderness

Intimation of Love?

Concert-goer

    And what what what is the Concert?

    Totality of appearances
    The evening vouchsafes
    And including
    Including

    A concert

Aesthete

All of his life drawn to it without understanding
Or even wondering
Wondering why

All of his life drawn to it without uncovering
Or even suspecting
A hidden presence

All of his life

Drawn to it

Puzzlement of a European

But how to account O just how to account
For my neighbour?

For what he sees
(Pictures and books)
For what he hears (symphonies and operas)
When all I can see
And when all I can hear
Is oppression
Exploitation

And murder?

Now

Companion perceiving in the street the Eternal
Young Man
Turned to me
And said:
'Beauty beauty his body once
But now his greeting's
Warmth
Desire desire to possess once
But now in affection
To grow
Pleasure pleasure of the flesh once
But now of completion
Of joyful completion

Of my pilgrimage'

Treasures in Heaven

And how does she lay them up?

By leaving the earth
And entering a room
By leaving sovereignty of moth rust and thieves
And entering
A room
Entering her study
Stanza where a Father awaits her words

'Treasures in heaven'
How does she lay them up?

By writing her poems

Saw You

'He shall drink of the brook in the way'

And so I did

Drank of the brook
Lifted up my head
And saw You

And the brook was Dominic's the way Tom's fourth
Nectar in C minor
Kirkpatrick one hundred
And thirty-nine

De torrente in via bibet

And so I did

Drank and drank deep
Lifted up my head
Unworthy head

And saw You!

Adam

No business of mine whatever You are
Apart from
My Maker
And apart from my Father whatever You may be
I've no wish
To know

Making me obliged You to remake Yourself
In my image

How else could You speak?
How else could we speak?

And how else could I love?

Steeple

    Tree in the landscape orchard's fugitive
    A tree
    In the land

    Tall as a cross and at a bend in the river
    With fruit to marvel at
    Shaped like a man
    Shaped like a boy
    And the man-fruit ripe drops into the river
    Boy-fruit ready
    Falls into the river

    And saves from drowning

New Name

Dying warrior to Christ: 'And shall I eat of the manna
Eat of the manna
And receive
The white stone?'

'Surely' replied the Lord

'And the name on the stone?'

'The one always written
The only inscribable
Your name shall be Salvation new name which you will bear

To your meeting'

A Twenty-sixth Set of Proverbs

i
Ugliest child New Continent born
Of Guilt

And of Self-loathing

ii
Said Democracy to her generals:
'Put this to a vote
And you'll lose
Lose
Put this to a vote and you'll most certainly lose
So quietly
Quietly

Just let it happen'

iii
And I said to the Painting in the European Museum:
'You mustn't worry

We're taking you with us'

iv
Winner visits London-in-the-Air
Loser

Lives in London-on-the-Ground

v
And Europe's ghost defiant
Cried:
'But see the mourners!
See the great crowd!

I live still!'

vi
Ugly before the informative talk
And ugly
Just as ugly

After

vii
Core
Core
Core of what we are:

The Mass

viii
What I wish you dearest dearest friend?
The young Giovan
Francesco and especially
His *San Guglielmo riceve l'abito*
Religioso
Da san Felice

Vescovo

ix
Olive in my grove nine hundred years old
As indeed

Am I

I Knelt Down Suddenly

And said:
'I who have written words
Who have written motion
Who have written words

Let me write silence
Let me write stillness
Write
Write

Your perfection!'

I Shall Wade Out

Until my thighs are steeped
In a burning resolve
To ask you Mr Cummings
You and other makers you and all makers
Of erotica:

'WHAT DO YOU THINK YOU ARE DOING?'

I Gazed Up at Stars

    Above a tree
    And gazed
    Gazed
    Gazed until I felt that Love which moves them
    Moves the stars
    Moves the tree
    Me
    All things

    And armed with this Love I walked home in perfect
    Peace in perfect
    Peace

    And contentment

Homecoming

    And we shall cleave to what we have done and seen
    Forgetting the melancholy
    Mysterious melancholy
    We shall cleave to what we have done and seen

    And the memory of those things
    Will make us gods
    Memory of those things irresistibly will make us

    Gods!

Late Poet

No one will ever be able to say of him:
'He fiddled
While Rome burned'

Powerless to prevent his city's destruction
(But how could he prevent it?
And who could expect?)
He nevertheless boldly confronted the flames
Nevertheless boldly
Confronted the fire

And condemned the fire-raisers

To a Lady

But the work is the man the work the man
That's what you fail
To understand
And when you learnt of the weightiest work
Of a particular man
You made no comment
None
At all

So be it
So be it
But what can we say of Silence your silence?
This we can say
This we can say:

That he begets Dissolution

To Monsieur Bonnard

      I love like you to sit in a house
      And gaze through an open
      Door to a garden
      To a garden and beyond to river and fields
      Yours in pigment
      And mine in words
      Our paintings are the same our paintings
      The same

      And what else do we do we sitters in a house
      Who gaze
      Through openness?
      What else do we do we sitters in a kitchen
      Who dream through an open
      Door

      Of Paradise?

To a Banana

Ripe little fruit I wish you to know
Before consumption
Before ingestion
That I do not regard you merely as a postulate
To explain
My experience

You are real and exist independently objectively
Are real and your substance
Is just
As I perceive

So depart in peace sweet little fruit!
Ripe little fruit
Good night

And thank you

Notes

Preface
Salmi 79.1.

Wrath of the Angel
Triggered by a passage in Douglas Murray's *The Strange Death of Europe*. Discussing in chapter 4 the African and Near Eastern migrants who arrive on the Italian island of Lampedusa, Mr Murray writes: 'Aside from the tiny number of earlier and better-off migrants, most people who arrive will eventually find themselves sleeping outside the train station in Milan or in a car park in Ravenna. The lucky ones will end up working for gangs or trying to sell imitation luxury goods on the bridges of Venice or down the side streets of Naples.'

Burning Tower
Although the Grenfell fire of 2017 occurred in London, relatively few of the victims were native British or European. The disaster provided further confirmation of the death of European society and culture. And that death is the true disaster.

Her Shame
Invocation here of the figure of Edmund Burke and of his view of society and culture.

A Twenty-second Set of Proverbs
I penned number v after hearing a performance of Haydn's *Applausus* cantata at the Cadogan Hall in Chelsea.

When Franz and Marie
In mid-August 1837 Liszt and his mistress, the Countess Marie d'Agoult, arrived in Como from Switzerland. Italy would be their home for the next two years and two months.

Out of the West
Job 2.12.

Eastern Maxim
Attributed to Mahatma Gandhi.

Response
The garden referred to is in Vienna, city of Sigmund Freud.

A Twenty-fourth Set of Proverbs
Number iv alludes to a monument in Ravenna and number vii to a *turba* chorus in Part Two of J. S. Bach's *St John Passion*.

The Dancer's Son
Apart from reference to a 'kerchief' Tolstoy does not describe what Natasha Rostov is wearing when, in Volume Two of *War and Peace*, she dances a folk-dance in her uncle's house. In the recent BBC dramatization of the book the actress playing Natasha (Lily James) wore a long, billowing, blue gown to perform the dance. The suggestion at this point in the novel is that Russia's peasant culture represents her true identity, an identity which Natasha, in spite of her aristocratic status, perfectly embodies.

Tolstoy's equally great contemporary, Dostoevsky, considered Russia spiritually superior to the West and the West's potential saviour.

Portrait by Lorenzo Lotto
   The sitter is probably Bartolomeo Carpan, a jeweller of Treviso and close friend of the artist.

Painting by Leonard McComb
   It featured in a retrospective of the artist's work in the Friends' Room of the Royal Academy, following Mr McComb's death in 2018.
   L.23: *Genesis* 2.10.

Portrait by Paul Cézanne
   Part of a recent, quite exceptional exhibition at London's National Portrait Gallery: *Cézanne: The Portraits*. The show illumined the gloomy winter months of 2017/18.
   'La fille aînée de l'Église' is a traditional title of France.
   The cathedral in Aix-en-Provence, Cézanne's native town, is dedicated to the Holy Saviour. My poem also refers to two other churches in Aix.

Line of T. S. Eliot
   In his *East Coker* of 1940.

Blue Poles
   I first saw Jackson Pollock's great work in the autumn of 2016, when it came to London for an Abstract Expressionist show at Burlington House. I had known the painting in reproduction for as long as I could remember.

A Twenty-fifth Set of Proverbs
   Number iii: rebellious Frankish noble of the late sixth century, murdered in the cathedral at Verdun.
   Number ix: César Soubeyran, character in Marcel Pagnol's novel of 1962, *Jean de Florette*. In chapter 2 he tells his nephew Ugolin ('Galinette') of his ambition to restore the family orchard to its former magnificence: «... ça, Galinette, ce serait un monument, ce serait beau comme une église, et

un vrai paysan n'y entrerait pas sans faire le signe de croix!»

Painted Chamber
Perhaps the supreme masterpiece of Andrea Mantegna: the Camera Picta or Camera degli Sposi in the Ducal Palace in Mantua.

Treasures in Heaven
Matthew 6.19–21.

Saw You
The quotation is from the closing verse of *Psalm 109*. My poem also refers to a keyboard sonata by Domenico Scarlatti and to the 'five ways of demonstrating God' of St Thomas Aquinas.

In the fourth of St Thomas's 'ways' intense meditation on a particular instance of beauty can disclose a beauty which is not particular but essential and absolute, Beauty itself, that perfect beauty which is God.

New Name
Revelation 2.17.

I Shall Wade Out
I first encountered E. E. Cummings' *i will wade out* in a setting for *a cappella* choir by the American composer Eric Whitacre. The music is very attractive, the poem notably less so.

I Gazed Up at Stars
Little homage to Dante, invoking the closing lines of the *Divina Commedia*.

To Monsieur Bonnard
In the spring of 2019 I made several visits to an exhibition at London's Tate Modern entitled *Pierre Bonnard: The Colour of Memory*.